WHALES
AND DOLPHINS

This edition produced in **1993** for
Shooting Star Press Inc
230 Fifth Avenue
New York, NY 10001

Design David West
Children's Book Design
Illustrations George Thompson
Picture Research C. Weston-Baker
Editor Denny Robson
Consultant John Stidworthy

© Aladdin Books Ltd 1988

Created and produced by
Aladdin Books Ltd
28 Percy Street
London W1P 9FF

*First published in the
United States in 1988 by*
Gloucester Press

ISBN 1-56924-003-5

Printed in Belgium

This book is about all the different types of whales — the baleen whales and the toothed whales, including porpoises and dolphins. The Identification Chart at the back of the book will show you their shapes and sizes and indicate the seas and oceans in which they live.

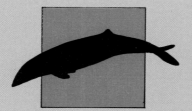

The little square shows you the size of the whale. Each side represents about 33ft (10m).

A red square means that the whale is an endangered species. See the Survival File.

A Humpback Whale leaps clear of the water ▷

FIRST SIGHT

WHALES
AND DOLPHINS

Lionel Bender

SHOOTING STAR PRESS

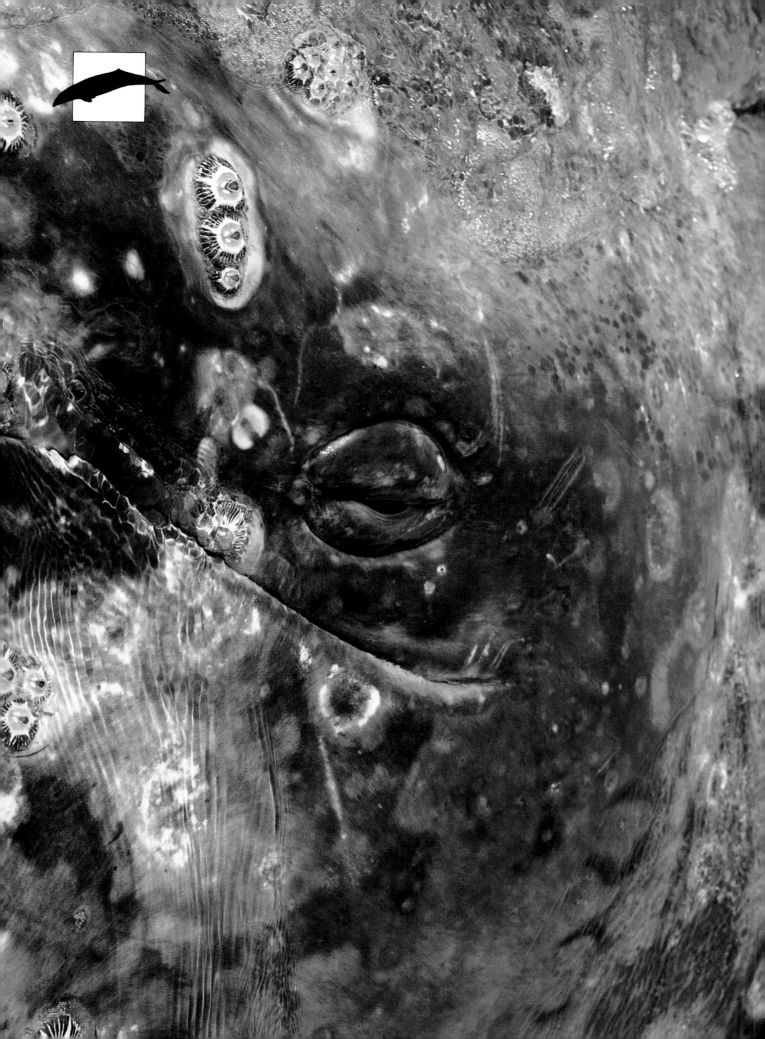

Introduction

Whales include the biggest animals ever known to exist. They also include the fastest swimmers alive. Some, like the Sperm Whale, descend to the ocean depths and are easily the deepest divers among the mammals. The small whales, the dolphins, are some of the most intelligent and playful of animals.

Whales enjoy being in groups and many are friendly toward people. But several kinds of whales have been hunted almost to extinction.

Because they live completely at sea, little is known about how many whales live. This book tells just some of the fascinating and surprising things known about these animals. Much more is still to be learned.

The picture opposite shows the head of a Gray Whale

Seagoing mammals

Although whales and dolphins resemble fish, they are in fact mammals like humans. They are warm blooded, they breathe air using lungs, and they give birth to live babies which feed on their mother's milk. Whales had ancestors that lived on land as most mammals do. But for the last 50 million years they have lived in the sea.

Like fish, whales are streamlined for swimming. But a whale swims by up and down movements of its tail, not side to side movements like a fish. Its front limbs are flippers, not fins. These have the same pattern of bones as we have in our arms and hands. The back limbs have disappeared over time. A whale's skin is smooth and has a few hairs while a fish has a scaly skin.

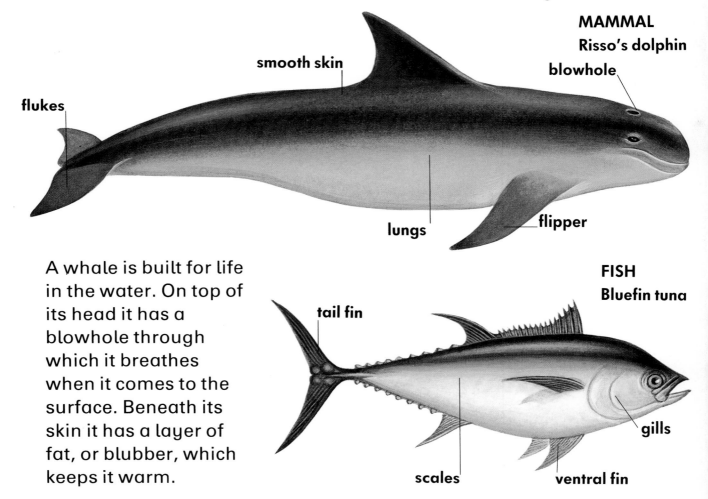

MAMMAL
Risso's dolphin

smooth skin

flukes

blowhole

lungs

flipper

A whale is built for life in the water. On top of its head it has a blowhole through which it breathes when it comes to the surface. Beneath its skin it has a layer of fat, or blubber, which keeps it warm.

FISH
Bluefin tuna

tail fin

scales

gills

ventral fin

6

Although 50ft (15m) long, the Humpback Whale glides easily through the water ▷

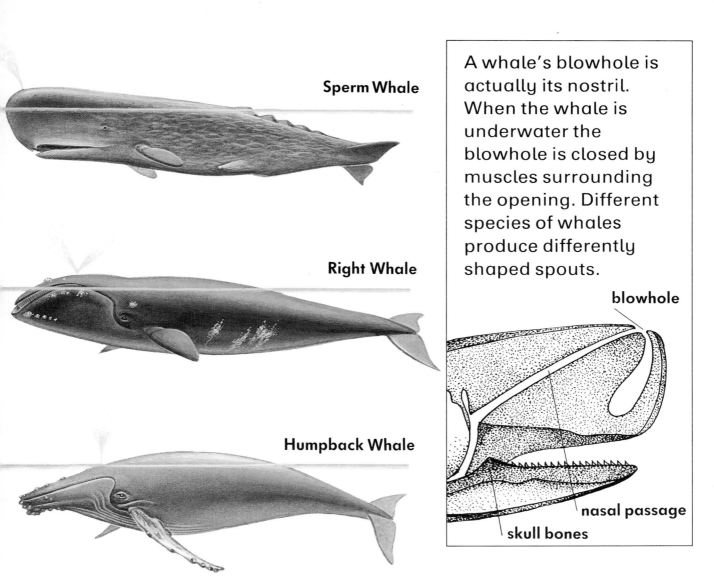

Sperm Whale

Right Whale

Humpback Whale

A whale's blowhole is actually its nostril. When the whale is underwater the blowhole is closed by muscles surrounding the opening. Different species of whales produce differently shaped spouts.

blowhole

nasal passage

skull bones

Breathing

Many whales can dive to great depths. A Sperm Whale can go down to more than 10,000 feet (3,000m) and stay underwater for 1½ hours at a time. Yet a whale must come to the surface to breathe. When it resurfaces, it pushes out used air through its blowhole, creating the familiar spout. It then takes a series of deep breaths before diving again.

In proportion to its body size, a whale's lungs are actually smaller than ours. But it fills its lungs much more fully than we do. A whale changes about 90 per cent of the air in its lungs at each breath, while we change only about 12 per cent. It also carries a supply of oxygen in its muscles.

◁ **The Blue Whale blows an upright spout up to 33 feet (10m) high**

Moving

Even huge species like the 50ft (15m) long Humpback Whale are natural acrobats and extremely agile swimmers. When they come up from a dive they may launch themselves completely out of the water and twist around in the air before crashing back through the surface. Dolphins often swim in groups in front of ships at sea, riding the bow waves like surfers.

Whales push themselves through the water by beating their tail flukes up and down with powerful body muscles. They use their flippers for steering. The water rushes easily over their smooth oily skin. They can change the shape of their body surface to cope with the huge water pressure deep in the sea.

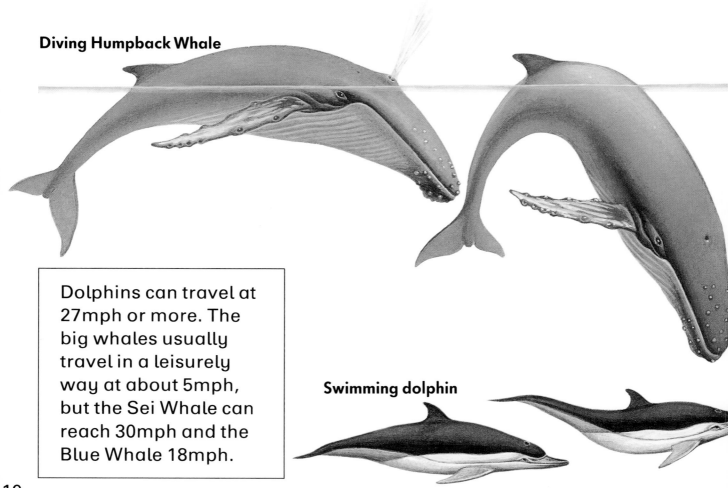

Diving Humpback Whale

Swimming dolphin

Dolphins can travel at 27mph or more. The big whales usually travel in a leisurely way at about 5mph, but the Sei Whale can reach 30mph and the Blue Whale 18mph.

△ **The Blue Whale's tail flukes are seen briefly as it dives**

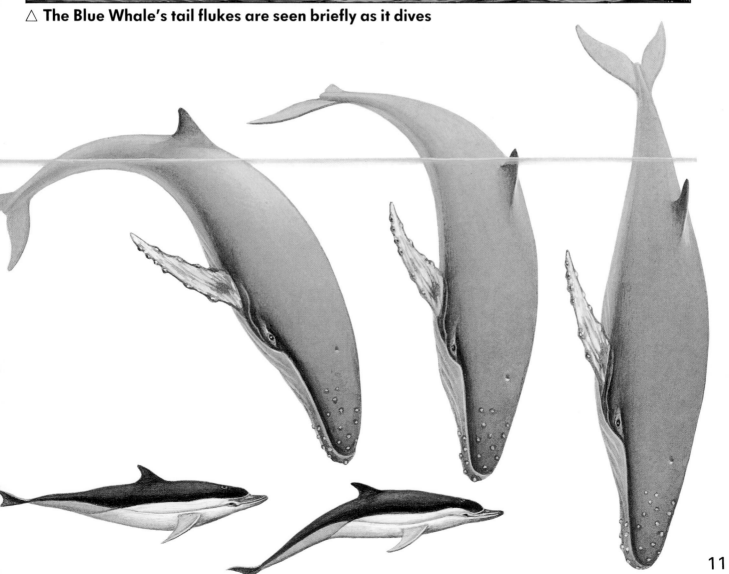

Baleen whales

There are two distinct groups of whales, the baleen and the toothed whales. There are ten species of baleen whales. Instead of teeth they have a series of horny plates with fringed edges hanging from the roof of the mouth. These whalebone plates are called the baleen and are used as a sieve for feeding.

Baleen whales feed on plankton – krill and other tiny creatures that float in the water. Where these swarm, the whale opens its mouth, takes in sea water, then pushes it out through the fringes. The food items are kept back by the fringes and then swallowed. The Blue Whale, the biggest animal that has ever lived, grows to 150 tons on this diet.

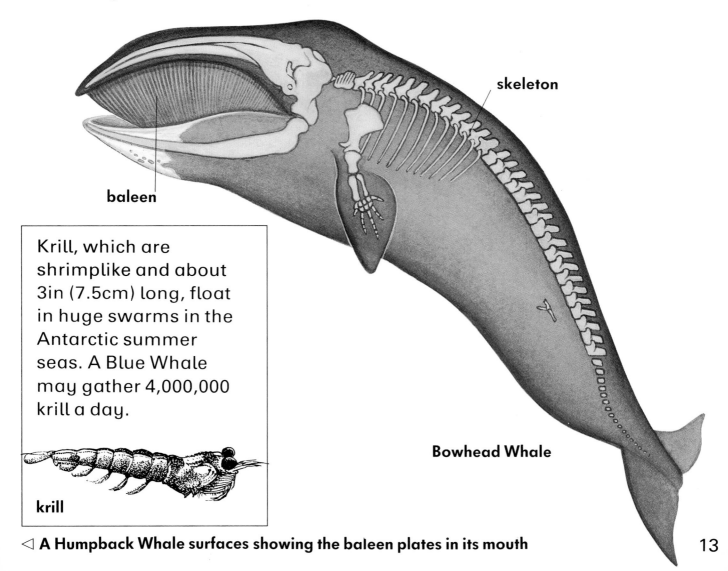

skeleton

baleen

Krill, which are shrimplike and about 3in (7.5cm) long, float in huge swarms in the Antarctic summer seas. A Blue Whale may gather 4,000,000 krill a day.

krill

Bowhead Whale

◁ **A Humpback Whale surfaces showing the baleen plates in its mouth**

Toothed whales

Most of the whales in the world, including all the dolphins, are toothed whales. They have jaw bones full of short cone-shaped teeth which they use to hold on to slippery prey like fish and squid. The Common Dolphin has more than 200 teeth. The Sperm Whale, and other species that feed on soft-bodied prey like squid, have less than 50.

The Killer Whale often eats warm-blooded prey such as penguins, seals and even dolphins. It hunts in packs with the whales working together as a team. Some dolphins, like the Bottlenose Dolphin, also feed as a group. They will round up and capture schools of fish such as tuna.

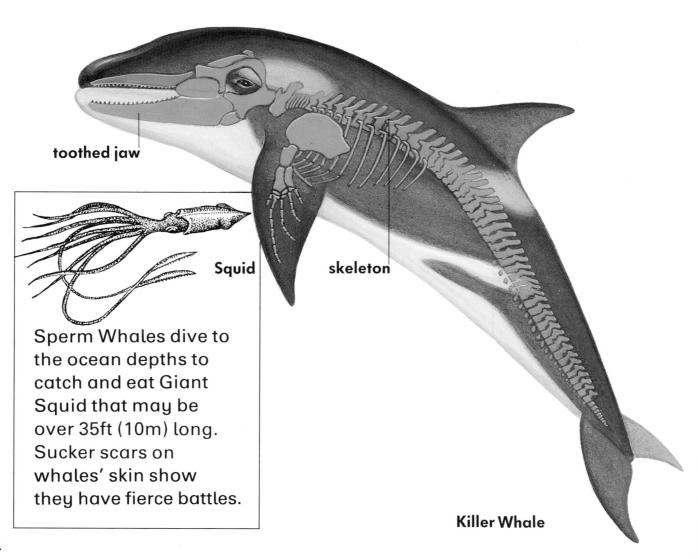

toothed jaw

Squid

skeleton

Sperm Whales dive to the ocean depths to catch and eat Giant Squid that may be over 35ft (10m) long. Sucker scars on whales' skin show they have fierce battles.

Killer Whale

Dolphins and porpoises

The smaller toothed whales include the unicorn-like Narwhal, the White Beluga, the dolphins and the porpoises. Porpoises have rounded heads, without the beak-like jaws that dolphins have. They grow to only about 5ft (1.5m) in length. They have a small top fin or none at all.

Dolphins can grow to about 13ft (4m) long and have a well-developed top fin. The Bottlenose Dolphin and the Common Dolphin are found almost worldwide, except for polar waters. River dolphins live in large tropical rivers like the Amazon and Indus. They are slow swimmers and sometimes use their long 'beak' to probe the river bed for crabs.

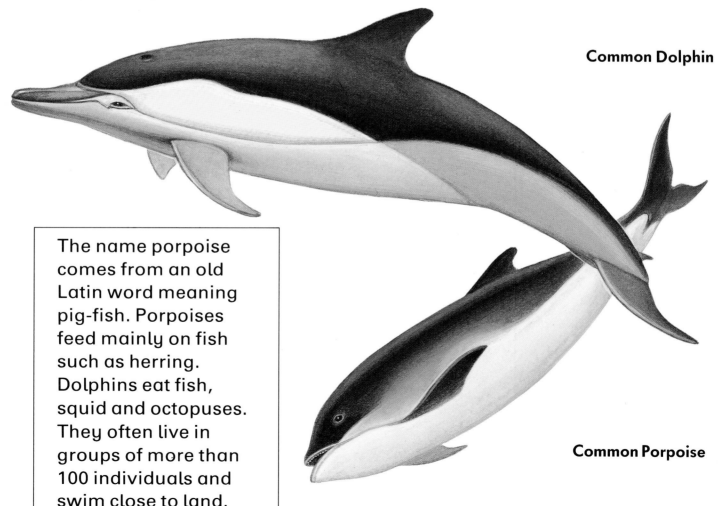

Common Dolphin

Common Porpoise

The name porpoise comes from an old Latin word meaning pig-fish. Porpoises feed mainly on fish such as herring. Dolphins eat fish, squid and octopuses. They often live in groups of more than 100 individuals and swim close to land.

16

The Bottlenose Dolphin prefers to live in groups ▷

Some whales use echolocation to navigate and to find prey. They make high-pitched sounds which are directed forward. Echoes bounce back from prey or the sea floor and are picked up by the whale's ears.

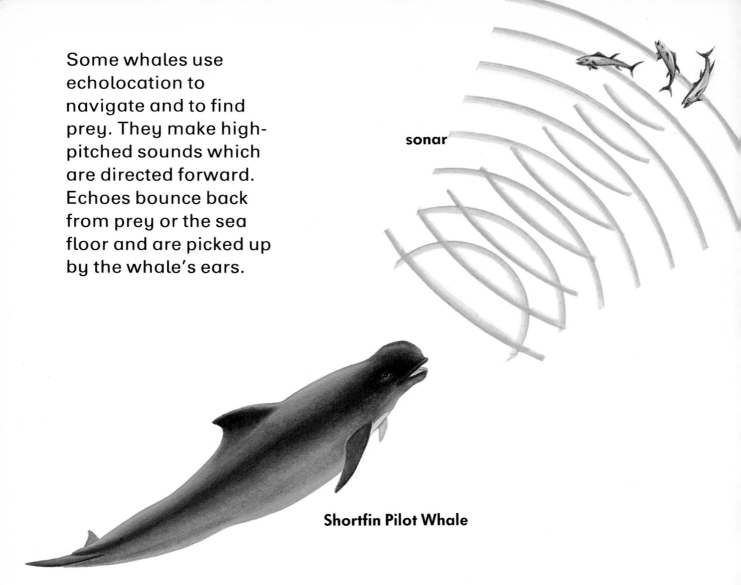

sonar

Shortfin Pilot Whale

Senses and sounds

Like humans, a whale has a pair of eyes and ears, a nose and a tongue. Whales can see quite well in open air and in shallow water. But because they do not have eyes that face forward, they cannot judge distances very well. When under water, a whale keeps its nostril closed and therefore cannot smell scents. But its tongue can taste chemicals in the water.

Whales do not have large ear openings. But they have excellent hearing and can detect sound waves traveling through the water. Whales make sounds that other whales can hear and respond to. Toothed whales navigate using echolocation, which is similar to the sonar used by ships to navigate.

Beluga Whales ('sea-canaries') have loud and varied voices ▷

Migration

Throughout the year most toothed whales are constantly on the move, following the schools of fish they feed on. This may take them on endless circuits around the oceans. By contrast, baleen whales make annual journeys back and forth between summer feeding and winter breeding areas.

The plankton on which baleen whales feed is most plentiful in Arctic and Antarctic waters during the summer. The Gray Whale migrates 12,500 miles from the far north to breeding grounds off California. Among Blue Whales, there are Northern and Southern Hemisphere populations. Their breeding grounds lie generally on either side of the Equator. The populations do not mix.

Migration route of the Gray Whale

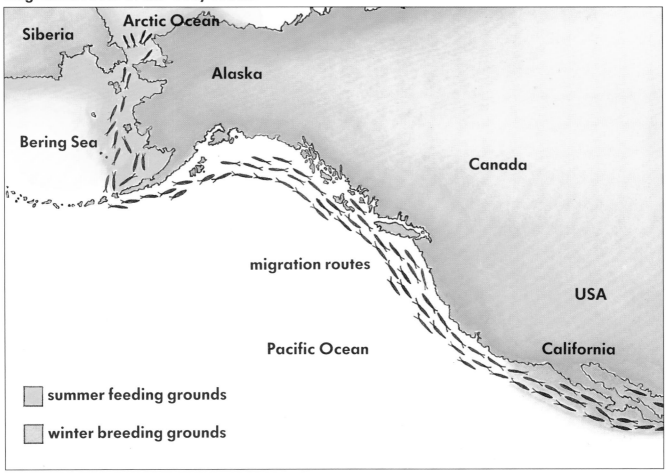

Siberia · Arctic Ocean · Alaska · Bering Sea · Canada · migration routes · USA · Pacific Ocean · California

☐ **summer feeding grounds**

☐ **winter breeding grounds**

◁ **Beluga Whales gather in huge herds as they move south in autumn**

A newborn dolphin has no air in its lungs and it tends to sink. Its mother, or her friends, nudge the baby to the surface where the air stimulates it to open its blowhole and take its first breath. After this it needs no more assistance to breathe or to feed.

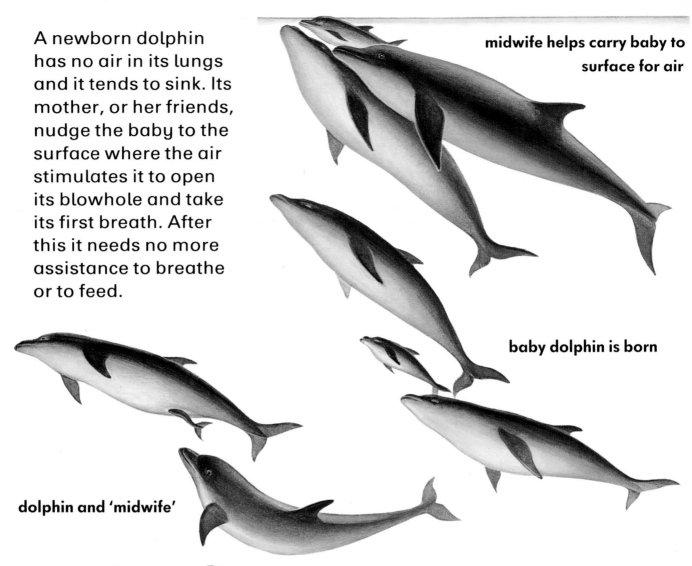

midwife helps carry baby to surface for air

baby dolphin is born

dolphin and 'midwife'

Breeding

Before mating, male toothed whales like the Sperm Whale often fight over females, butting and biting each other for the right to mate. Males of all species usually court the females. They chase them through the water, perform displays of splashing and diving, then swim alongside and stroke and caress them with their head. Even large species like the Humpback Whale have energetic courtship displays, ending with the pair rising out of the water to mate face to face.

In baleen whales, courtship and mating take place in warm tropical waters and the young are born there the following year. In most whales pregnancy lasts for about a year.

A male Gray Whale courts a female under water ▷

Giant babies

Whales have the biggest babies in the world – a Blue Whale calf may be 24ft (7.6m) long and weigh 15,400 lbs (7,000 kg). They are also some of the fastest growing young, doubling their weight in the first week. The calves eat for the first time a few minutes after birth. When the mother suckles the calf, she pumps milk into its mouth which is very thick and rich in fat.

In big baleen whales like the Humpback, Blue and Gray, the mothers produce milk for about six months. By this time the whales have returned to the summer polar feeding grounds where the young can easily find plankton food. The mother can then replace the blubber that she converted to milk.

◁ **A baby Humpback Whale and its mother**

The Blue Whale may weigh as much as 7 tons at birth. It grows rapidly at first. Growth slows as it reaches maturity.

1 day (24ft; 7.5m)

7 months (53.3ft; 16m)

5 years old (76.5ft; 23m)

25 years old (86.5ft; 26m)

By swimming close to its mother a baby whale gets an easier ride ▷

Intelligence

Dolphins appear to be highly intelligent. They have a language of whistles, chirps, clicks and moans that allows them to communicate with one another over great distances. In captivity they learn tricks and are able to copy many sounds and actions made by people. Some scientists believe that they are more intelligent than dogs, but less so than apes.

Some of a whale's intelligent behavior may just be the result of natural playfulness and friendliness rather than true intelligence. Female whales, for example, automatically help one another to bring up their calves. Dolphins automatically help other injured dolphins to the surface to breathe.

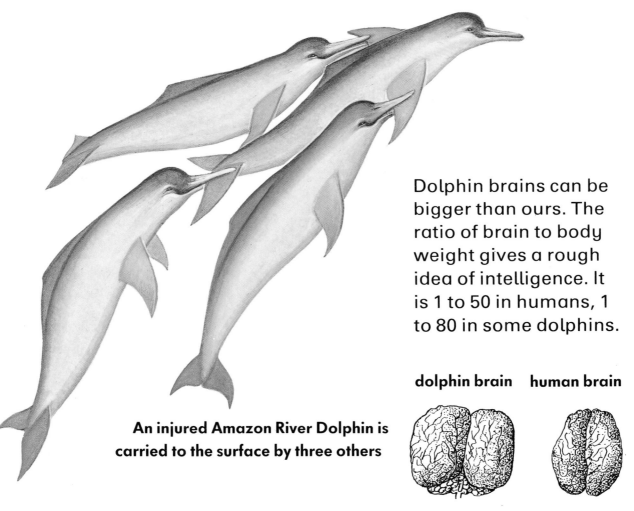

Dolphin brains can be bigger than ours. The ratio of brain to body weight gives a rough idea of intelligence. It is 1 to 50 in humans, 1 to 80 in some dolphins.

An injured Amazon River Dolphin is carried to the surface by three others

dolphin brain   **human brain**

◁ **Dolphins can communicate by sounds**

Survival file

For hundreds of years whales have been hunted and killed. Their flesh is still eaten by many people around the world and is also used to make pet foods. Blubber is the source of whale oil that can be used as a fuel. Smokeless candles, lamps and a lubricant oil for machines can also be made from whale products. The whaling industry has been a ruthless destroyer of wildlife. The numbers of many species have dropped dramatically as animals have been killed faster than they can breed. Today whaling is being halted to let populations grow again.

Whales and dolphins are being studied by scientists

The Right Whales were the first to become rare as they were the "right" (easiest) whales to hunt. Being slow swimmers, they were easily caught by the first sailboat whaling ships. With the development of engine-powered whaling ships and explosive harpoons, all whales became easy targets for the hunters. Then it was the Sperm Whale and the big baleen whales that suffered. In 1931 thirty thousand Blue Whales were killed in the Antarctic. Never again have so many been seen. There are probably little more than ten thousand left in the whole world.

Dolphins are also hunted for meat in some parts of Southeast Asia and South America. Many others die trapped in fishing nets.

Conservation measures and falling profits have brought whaling to a standstill in certain countries. But whaling still continues in other parts of the world. For many species numbers have fallen so low that their recovery is now in doubt. Often little is known about how they live. It is only in the last thirty years that dolphins and small whales have been studied in captivity.

The explosive harpoon made it easier to catch and kill big whales

Killer Whales in a marine park

Identification chart

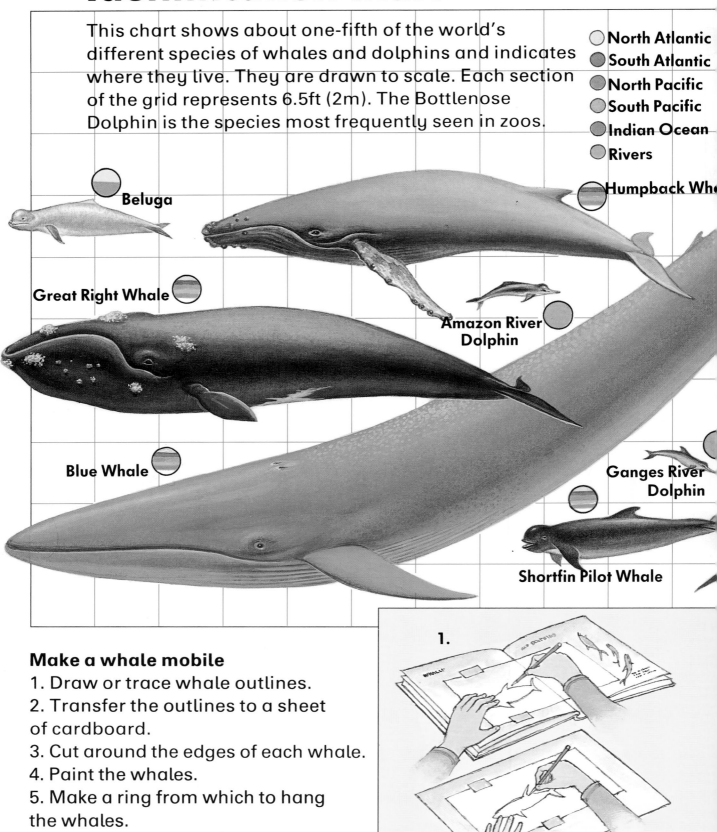

This chart shows about one-fifth of the world's different species of whales and dolphins and indicates where they live. They are drawn to scale. Each section of the grid represents 6.5ft (2m). The Bottlenose Dolphin is the species most frequently seen in zoos.

○ North Atlantic
◑ South Atlantic
◔ North Pacific
◐ South Pacific
◑ Indian Ocean
○ Rivers

Humpback Wh

Beluga

Great Right Whale

Amazon River Dolphin

Blue Whale

Ganges River Dolphin

Shortfin Pilot Whale

Make a whale mobile
1. Draw or trace whale outlines.
2. Transfer the outlines to a sheet of cardboard.
3. Cut around the edges of each whale.
4. Paint the whales.
5. Make a ring from which to hang the whales.
6. Using thread, attach the whales to the ring and the ring to the ceiling.

1.

2.

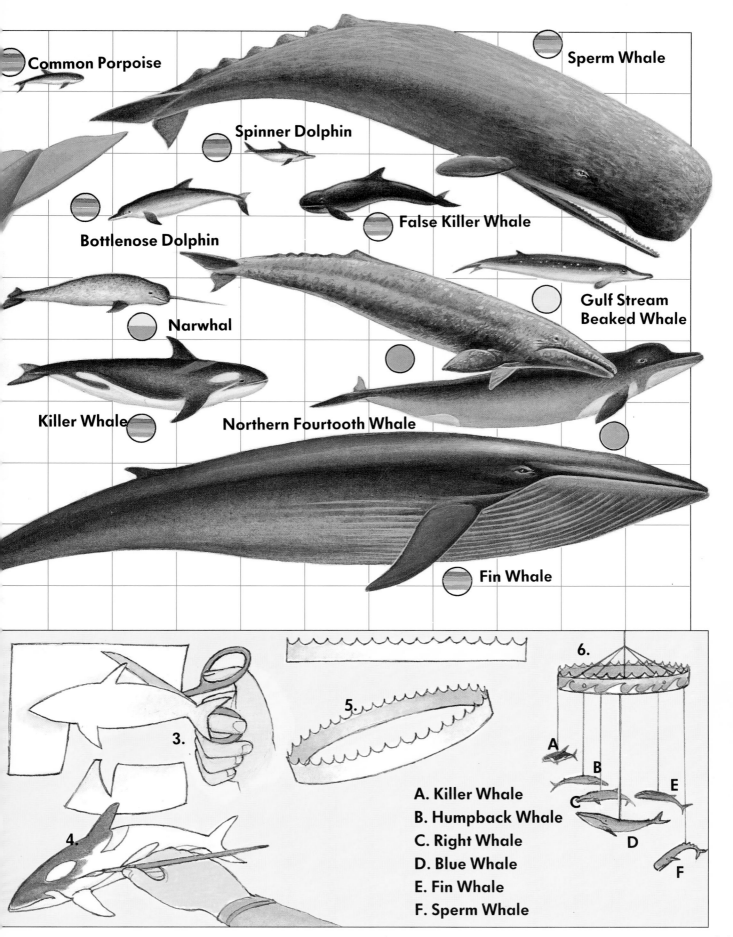

Common Porpoise

Sperm Whale

Spinner Dolphin

Bottlenose Dolphin

False Killer Whale

Narwhal

Gulf Stream Beaked Whale

Killer Whale

Northern Fourtooth Whale

Fin Whale

3.

5.

6.

A. Killer Whale
B. Humpback Whale
C. Right Whale
D. Blue Whale
E. Fin Whale
F. Sperm Whale

4.

31

Index

Photographic Credits:
Title page: Zefa; intro
and pages 11, 17 and
19: Ardea; pages 7, 12,
23, 24, 26 and 29: Planet
Earth; pages 8, 15, 28
and 29: Bruce Colman;
pages 20, 25 and 28
(inset): Survival Anglia.